Car...

D0832242

Donner Party

A Diary of a Survivor

Tod Olson

SCHOLASTIC INC.
New York Toronto London Auckland Sydney
Mexico City New Delhi Hong Kong Buenos Aires

Illustrations by
Matt Collins

The text in this edition has been revised from the original edition.

ISBN 0-439-66706-2

SCHOLASTIC, READ 180, and associated logos and designs are trademarks and/or registered trademarks of Scholastic Inc.

LEXILE is a registered trademark of MetaMetrics, Inc.

9   10   23   12 11 10 09

Contents

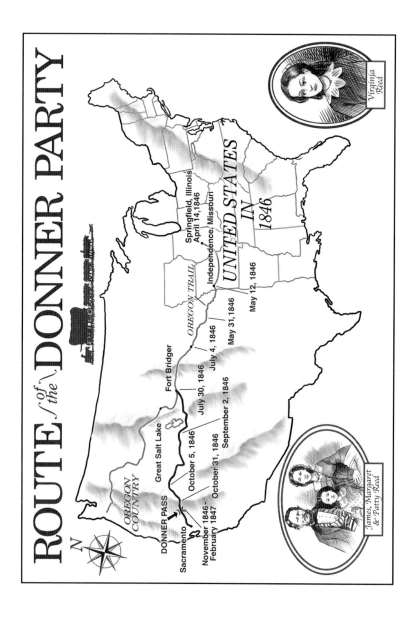

ROUTE of the DONNER PARTY

N

UNITED STATES
IN
1846

OREGON COUNTRY

OREGON TRAIL

Springfield, Illinois
April 14, 1846

Independence, Missouri

May 12, 1846

May 31, 1846

July 4, 1846

July 30, 1846

Fort Bridger

Great Salt Lake

October 5, 1846

October 31, 1846

September 2, 1846

DONNER PASS

Sacramento

November 1846 -
February 1847

Virginia Reed

James, Margaret
& Patty Reed

Virginia Reed dreamed of going West. But her trip became a nightmare.

Introduction

This story is gross. But it's true.

More than 150 years ago, groups of people were headed West. They were hoping to start new lives. Many were looking for good farmland. And they had heard that there was lots of it in California.

One of these groups was called the Donner Party. It was named after two brothers who planned the trip. There were about 100 people in this group.

The Donner Party left from Springfield, Illinois. They started west in April 1846. By August, they had traveled more than 1,000 miles. They had crossed dry **plains**, hot deserts, and high mountains.

And they had walked much of the way.

They were getting closer. But then, in the fall, it started to snow. Snow covered their trail. They had to stop and wait for the snow to stop.

But the snow didn't stop. And soon, the group ran out of food. People dropped dead. People who **survived** ate ox **hides**. Then they ate their dogs. Then there was nothing at all to eat. Nothing.

Except the dead bodies.

What do you think they did?

You're about to find out.

One of the people in this group was a girl named Virginia Reed. She was 12 years old. You're about to read her diary. This diary is **fiction**. But it is based on fact.

We're close to California. We decide to take a shortcut. But it isn't short at all.

1 Shortcut

July 31, 1846. We left Fort Bridger today. Papa, Mama, little Patty, and I are traveling with 23 other wagons. I ride Billy, my pony. Cash the dog walks next to us.

My family has three wagons. Twenty **oxen** pull them. Papa and Milt Elliott and Baylis Williams drive our oxen.

The men in the group are arguing. One says we will be buried in snow before we reach California. I'm sure he's just nervous. Winter is far away. It is so hot that I had to find a tree for shade. And besides, Papa says he knows of a **shortcut**.

I cannot wait to get to California. My

friend John says he will find gold. He'll share it with me. And we'll live like kings.

August 3. We met riders coming east. They warned us not to take the shortcut. But Papa says he read that the trail is good.

Four oxen are dead from drinking dirty water. Their bellies were full like balloons.

August 12. I cannot ride my pony. We're in a thick forest. There is no trail. We must make our own trail as we go.

The men cut down trees and bushes. They move huge rocks out of the way.

We go one or two miles every day. Time goes as slowly as our wagon wheels.

August 20. We have spent three weeks on the shortcut. Papa said it would take only one. The men say that Papa chose the wrong trail. One man said Papa will be a murderer if anyone dies.

The desert steals everything we own. And it almost takes our lives.

2 Desert Days

September 1, 1846. We made it through the forest. Now we have to cross a desert. We are resting near a big, salty lake. The men are packing grass into the wagons. We don't want the cattle to starve.

September 5. We've spent two days in the desert. Still we cannot see the end. The day is as hot as a frying pan. At night we freeze.

We do not have enough water. My tongue is big and dry, like a rag in my mouth.

Patty was crying for water. Papa yelled at her. Then he felt bad.

All the oxen ran away to find water. Now there are none left to pull the wagons. So we left the wagons behind.

My pony Billy has dropped to the ground. His tongue hangs into the sand.

September 6. We have walked all night. I'm lying with Mama and Patty. The dogs are our blankets. It's so cold. I'm too weak to write.

September 8. We are resting at a water hole. We found six of our oxen here. So we went back and got one wagon. We are leaving most of our things behind.

Mama kept her **shawl** and left her mirror. I kept my diary and left my summer hat. I kept my Bible and left my leather shoes. Papa says we will come back and get everything. But I never want to see this place again.

We left Billy lying dead in the sand.

Papa is thrown out of the group. And our hope goes with him.

3 Murder!

September 13, 1846. We are finally out of the desert.

There is not much food left. We sit down to weak soup at breakfast. We eat dried beef and biscuits at night.

Papa went hunting yesterday. He caught one skinny rabbit. I know he is worried. Still, he tries to cheer us up. He says we will soon eat fresh fruit and meat in California.

A storm came last night and dropped lots of snow on the hills.

October 5. I thought we had seen trouble in the desert! But we didn't know. . . .

I must be calm and tell what happened. A man named John Snyder was pushing his oxen up a steep hill. He was beating his cattle with a whip.

Father saw him do it. He told Snyder to stop. "The animals are our only hope," he said. "And we have so few left." They argued. Then Snyder hit father with his whip handle.

Mama stepped in. John Snyder hit her, too. Papa pulled out his hunting knife and stabbed Snyder. Snyder fell to the ground. He is dead. Now some of the men want Papa to be hanged!

October 6. Father has been thrown out.

He had only a skinny horse to ride. He didn't have much food. So, after dark, John and I rode after him. I gave him some dried meat. I threw my arms around him. He said he would make it to California. Then he would bring us food. But I don't know. . . .

We try to get to California before winter.
Then fear makes us all act like animals.

4   Racing the Snow

October 8, 1846. Our oxen move slowly. Their ribs push against their skin. My dog Cash barks and bites at their ankles. But they move so slowly, like snails.

Each day we pass things that people have left on the trail. Today I saw a desk, a family's Sunday clothes, and some toys.

Sometimes I just want to lie down on the trail. I want to give up. I don't care if I ever get to California.

October 9. An old man named Hardkoop couldn't keep up with the group. So he dropped behind. We think he is dead.

October 12. We're in a **marsh** now. The ground is wet and muddy. It smells like dead things. After this marsh, there's another desert. After that, there are the Sierra Nevada mountains. We are in a race with snow and hunger.

John's pony fell into a **bog**. No one would help us pull it out. It twisted and splashed. Then it disappeared.

October 18. Every day we get closer to the mountains. On the other side is California. I would give anything to get there.

Snow fell again, ahead of us. The mountains in front of us are turning white.

Virginia says that they're "in a race with snow and hunger." What does she mean?

We've come so close . . . but our dreams are sunk in an ocean of snow.

5 Trapped!

October 28, 1846. Now, snow is everywhere. First it came in tiny, wet flakes. I thought of Christmas. Now it feels like knives. Every flake stings my face. We move so slowly.

October 31. We are buried in white. I sink to my waist. Every step is hard work. I wait. Then I take another step. All day I hear the cries of mothers, babies, and men.

November 1. We have set fire to a tall pine. I am writing by its light. I pray no more snow comes tonight.

November 2. When I slept last night, John stood under a tree. He was wrapped in a blanket. When I awoke he was still there. He was covered in white. All night he stood, just watching.

This morning it was decided. We cannot go on. We must build **huts**. And we must try to find food. We will be here until the snow melts.

I pray that we can last that long.

Do you think that the group has made a good decision? Or is this the beginning of the end?

We make a home in the mountains. And we try to hang on.

6 Snowed In

November 11, 1846. For a week, it has snowed. We have built four log huts. We made the roofs from animal hides. There are fireplaces made of rocks inside.

Sixty people are here. The Donners and some others are nearby.

Mama bought two cattle from a man named Mr. Graves. She promised to pay him when we get to California. We killed the cattle and buried the meat in the snow. It will freeze there. That will keep it from going bad.

November 27. White. It's the color of clean sheets, clouds, potatoes, cream, and the meat of a turkey. Now when the sun is out, everything is white. White burns my eyes. I never want to see white again.

December 12. It snows every day. Sometimes we cannot go out for days. We shovel snow out of the fireplace each morning. We chip wood from the sides of the cabin. Then we burn it. My hands get warm if I hold them close to the fire. But deep inside, I'm always cold. I shake so much. I hope someone will be able to read this.

December 13. Baylis Williams is sick. He drove our oxen 1,800 miles. It is only 100 more miles to California. John tried to give him food today. He cannot eat.

December 15. Baylis Williams is dead. We buried him in a mound of snow. I once thought heaven was all white. Now I'm sure it's not.

We run out of food. And we try to get over the mountains.

7 Life or Death

December 30, 1846. A man named Charley died today. Someone grabbed his money, watch, and jewelry. Another took his coat and clothes. They left his body in the snow.

January 2, 1847. Our beef is gone. We can't last much longer. Patty cries for food all morning. Then she's silent the rest of the day.

January 4. Mama, Milt Elliott, and I are leaving. Patty will die if we do not find some meat. I said good-bye to our dog Cash. John tried to give me some food. But I know he needs to eat, too. So I did not take it.

January 5. Milt leads the way on snowshoes. We follow. I try to walk on top of the snow. But I fall through. A leg disappears. I pull it out. I start to crawl.

January 6. My feet are very cold. They hurt so much. I have to crawl most of the day.

At night, Milt gets wood and builds a fire. He puts green logs on the bottom. That way the fire won't burn through the snow.

I found beef in my sack tonight. I am sure it's from John.

January 9. The mountain almost killed us. We are back at the cabin.

Two nights ago, we awoke in a deep hole. The fire had burned through the snow, and we had fallen. When we woke up, we were ten feet down. We had to cut steps to get out.

Now I'm sitting at the fire. I'm warming my frozen feet.

All our food is gone. We try to eat ox hides. Can it get any worse?

8 **Starving**

January 12, 1847. There's nothing left to eat. Mama took an ox hide from our roof. She boiled it on the fire. It turned into a thick paste. Mama put the mess onto our plates. I closed my eyes. I tried to pretend it was stew. But I could not eat it.

January 30. Mr. Graves took away our hides yesterday. We bought cattle from him weeks ago. He took the hides as payment. His daughters are starving. We have only two hides left. And we have no roof at all. John's father has taken us in.

February 6. I cannot eat the hides. But there is nothing else. I fear I will die. We sit at night by the fire and pray. It is all we can do. Milt is even weaker than I am.

February 8. Each night, John gives me half his food. It is a piece of beef as small as a coin. He looks at me. His mouth smiles. But his eyes do not.

February 9. Tonight we will eat Cash. John's father killed him with a knife. He is cooking him on the fire. The smell makes my mouth water. We will eat him in small pieces. He will feed us for three days.

I can't believe this is happening.

February 14. Milt has died. We buried him in the snow. First we covered his feet and legs. Then we covered the rest of him. He is just a mound of snow. I hate to imagine what this awful place will be like when the snow melts.

February 15. Wolves dug up a body last night. It wasn't Milt. The wolves dragged the body into the woods. Then they ate it. People here say we should do the same.

February 18. People here are talking about digging up Milt. But no one has done it. I cannot do it myself.

But what if someone else did it?

I cannot say I would not eat.

If you were starving, and the only thing to eat was a dead person, what do you think you would do?

People arrive from California to save us. And we fight the snow again.

9 **Relief!**

February 19, 1847. Yesterday, John heard a shout. He ran outside. Then he yelled back to us. "They're here! Thank God! They're finally here!"

Seven men from California have come to help us. And they have brought some food.

February 21. Mama, Patty, and I are leaving with the men. Only the strongest of us can go. There will be 23 of us.

John and his family are staying. It is terrible to see their faces. Other people will come to help. But I couldn't stay here one more day.

February 23. Will this mountain ever let us go? Patty cannot keep walking. Someone is taking her back to the camp. Mama wanted to go with her. But Patty said, "Please go find Papa."

We watched the people carry Patty away.

February 24. During the day, we walk. At night, we lie on the snow and sleep. When we awake, our clothes are frozen. We walk again. The sun melts the ice. Then our clothes are heavy, cold, and wet.

I am too weak to walk. I must crawl over each mound of snow. Mama stays ahead of me. She tells me we are getting closer to Papa. And she says there will soon be more food.

What do you think will happen to Virginia and her mother?

We are a family again—in California.

10 Papa!

February 27, 1847. Today I felt like giving up. Then we heard shouts from ahead. "Is Mrs. Reed with you? Tell her Mr. Reed is here!" Mama fell on the snow. I tried to run. I fell, too. Then I looked up. Papa was there. His pockets were full of bread.

February 28. Papa is going back to get Patty. We have full bellies and new hope. Maybe now we can escape this white jail.

March 21. We are a family again. Papa is back. Patty is in bed. She can only drink soup and eat small bits of bread.

Papa had a horrible tale to tell. He reached Patty in two days. He left with her and 15 others. But terrible snowstorms nearly buried them all alive. They had nothing to eat for four days.

Then three people died. The others knew they could die, too. They had no choice. They had to eat the dead to stay alive. I was shocked at first. But I knew I might do the same.

April 8. I am sitting in a meadow. John is next to me. We're eating lamb, fresh-baked bread, and sweet grapes. Green is everywhere, green grass, green trees. I could sit here forever—in California.

Glossary

bog *(noun)* wet land

fiction *(noun)* a story that is not true

hides *(noun)* animal skin

huts *(noun)* small, simple houses

marsh *(noun)* wet, low land

oxen *(noun)* adult male cattle. They are used as work animals, or for beef.

plains *(noun)* large, flat areas of land

shawl *(noun)* a piece of clothing that is worn over the shoulders

shortcut *(noun)* a faster way to get somewhere

survived *(verb)* lived through a horrible event